isl

Short ∧ Walks on Dartmoor

Paul White

Bossiney Books · Launceston

Other Bossiney Walks Books
Really short walks north Dartmoor
Really short walks south Dartmoor
Shortish walks in north Cornwall
Shortish walks in north Devon
Shortish walks near the Land's End
Shortish walks on Exmoor
Shortish walks – St Ives to Padstow
North Dartmoor pub walks
South Dartmoor pub walks

This reprint 2006. First published 2003 by
Bossiney Books Ltd, Langore, Launceston, Cornwall PL15 8LD
www.bossineybooks.com
ISBN 1-899383-60-3

Acknowledgements
The maps are by Graham Hallowell, cover design by Heards Design Partnership,
photographs by the author
Printed in Great Britain by R Booth Ltd, Mabe, Cornwall

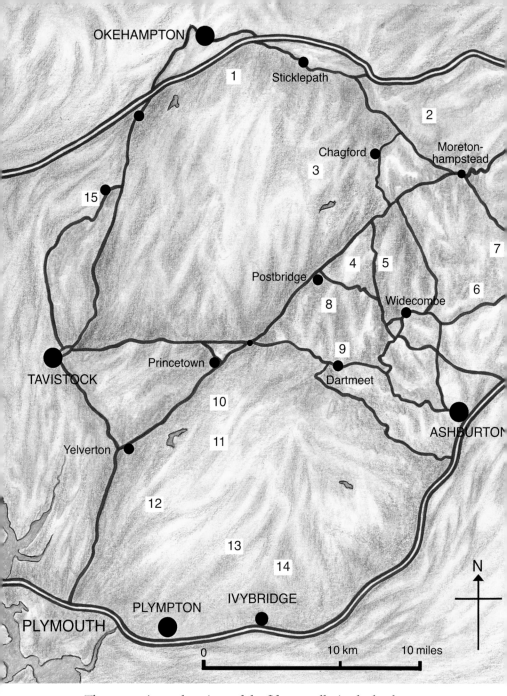

The approximate locations of the fifteen walks in the book

Introduction

These 'shortish' walks are typically 5-8 km (3-5 miles) and will take a morning or an afternoon. The exact time will vary according to your fitness, weather conditions, and above all how interested you are in what you see. The 'duration of walk' times make no allowance for this as it is such a variable: it would be quite possible on some of the walks to spend another hour investigating the sites you pass through.

Safety (please take seriously!)

Like any hill area, Dartmoor can at times be tricky, even dangerous. I don't want to be over-dramatic: you will probably have no problems, but some of these walks take you into exposed and lonely places where mobile phones get no reception. You need to go prepared.

Dartmoor weather can change abruptly. The 'low cloud' which mars a morning on the beach is experienced by walkers on the moor as thick fog. Apart from the risk of getting disorientated, the temperature drops abruptly. Always take more layers of warm clothing than you expect to need: the high moor will always be colder than the lowland; you need another spare layer *as well as* waterproofs in your rucksack. On the high moor you should carry water with you (dehydration makes you tired) and some spare food.

I recommend you *always* carry a compass for these walks as a safety measure: in a few cases the instructions actually require a compass. And the sketch maps we provide are just that, sketches: the Ordnance Survey's 1:25,000 map of Dartmoor, Outdoor Leisure 28, is absolutely essential and very good value. You need proper walking boots or shoes for grip and ankle support – and even after a month without rain (rare!) some parts of all these walks will be soggy underfoot.

Access

Access is generally allowed to unenclosed parts of Dartmoor (except the military ranges, which this book avoids entirely) but walkers have no right to walk over enclosed land except on footpaths, or where there is an 'access agreement'. So please keep to the paths, close gates as appropriate, keep dogs fully under control, and respect the needs of those whose livelihood depends on the moor.

I hope you will enjoy the walks and come to love Dartmoor as much as I have.

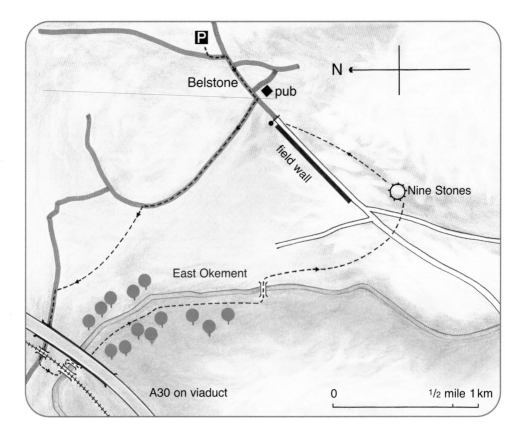

Walk 1 Belstone West Cleave and the Nine Stones circle

Distance: 6.5 km   Duration of walk: 1³/4 hours
Character: Initially farmland, then woodland beside a fast-running river, then open moorland.

Start at the Belstone village car park (621938) and walk into the village, which is very pretty with much stone and thatch. Notice the stocks and the pound, now a garden. And the Tors pub awaiting your return. Pass the 'telegraph office' and bear right along a tarmac lane – no sign post, but to the right of fire hydrant 3SV22.

After 1 km cross a cattle grid and within 15 m turn left across a stile. Cross the field and pass through a derelict gateway, then bear right alongside a field boundary. At the bottom right corner of the field is a further stile. Cross it, follow the hedge to your left downhill and over yet another stile – this time with removable wooden bars – until you reach a stream where a path leads across a simple bridge and out onto a minor lane – its sheltered banks providing a haven for wild flowers, especially in late spring. Turn left along it.

4

*Belstone
Nine Stones*

Cross under the A30 and then under the railway line, turning left at the road junction. Turn left again past a car parking area (an alternative start for the walk) through a gate and under the railway viaduct. Then turn right across a footbridge over the East Okement River, left through a gate, and back under the A30.

Follow the path nearest the river, which rushes down a steep descent across granite rapids. In places the path goes very near the river and you should be very cautious if the river is likely to be in flood.

You will reach a wooden footbridge crossing a tributary. Cross. The path leads to a hidden gap in the wall ahead. From here the path is uneven in places. This is a good place for bluebells in the spring.

Some 200 m beyond a small but attractive waterfall, join another path and continue up the valley. Then cross the river by a footbridge (at 608934) and turn right. You are now on open moorland. On the skyline ahead of you you will see a substantial tor – Belstone Tor – and you need gradually to head in that direction following a path which leads up from the valley floor. When the path gives out, continue heading for Belstone Tor, the highest point around you. In due course you will reach a well-made track (611927). Turn left. After perhaps 100 m (depending on where you joined the track exactly), bear off at 45° to the right, up a fairly well defined minor path, and you will come to another track. Cross this and you should be able to see 100 m or so ahead of you the Nine Stones cairn circle – which contains 16 stones!

At the circle, turn your back on Belstone Tor and walk in a straight line till you reach a track. Turn right along it. Head for the stone wall and follow the track through a gate. The road will take you back down into Belstone village.

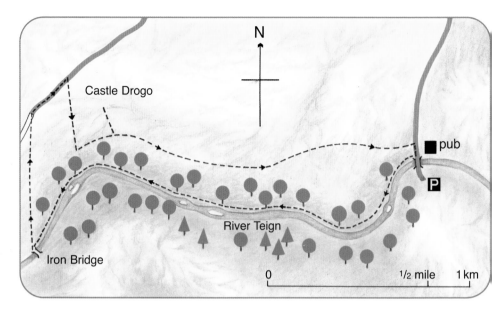

Walk 2 Fingle Bridge

Distance: 6.5 km   Duration of walk: nearly 2 hours
Character: Delightful woodland, then views over wooded valley.

Assuming your vehicle is thin enough, cross Fingle Bridge and park in the car park on the far side, where incidentally there are toilets.

Cross back over the bridge and turn left through the kissing gate opposite the Fingle Bridge Inn (formerly the Angler's Rest). You will follow this so-called FISHERMAN'S PATH along the River Teign, at varying heights above the water, for nearly 2 km. Both sides of the gorge are covered in mostly deciduous woodland, with outcropping rocks.

The path is mainly smooth, but there are occasional flights of steps with deep risers, and exposed tree roots; some walkers may find it quite difficult. It is, however, extremely beautiful. All along the bank there is evidence that the river floods in winter and erodes the soil, including the path. Don't attempt the walk if the river is in flood.

One landmark is a massive outcrop of rock immediately above the path. About 100 m beyond this is the site of the Iron Bridge, which at the time of writing was not in position, but about to be replaced.

Where the Iron Bridge should be, you turn right, signed 'HUNTER'S PATH AND ROAD NEAR CASTLE DROGO'. This path is part of the Two Moors Way. As it climbs it passes a beautiful old farm on the left and then joins a tarmac track. Follow this for 400 m, then turn right along a path which leads back at a sharp angle, taking you into the Castle Drogo estate.

Fingle Bridge, the starting point for this walk

This path climbs steadily but gently up the side of the valley, revealing for the first time the distant views of the higher moor, then does a dog-leg to the left, giving a splendid view down the gorge which you have just traversed.

After several hundred metres, two separate paths lead off on the left to the fascinating National Trust property, Castle Drogo, and its garden, but our walk carries straight on. Cross Piddledown Common and you will find yourself standing on top of Sharp Tor, again with magnificent views.

Gorse and silver birch predominate along this 'HUNTER'S PATH'. Bear right at the fork in the path and descend to Fingle Bridge and your car.

If you are looking for somewhere for lunch, there is of course the Fingle Bridge Inn immediately to hand, or in nearby Drewsteignton there is a famously characterful old pub, the Drewe Arms.

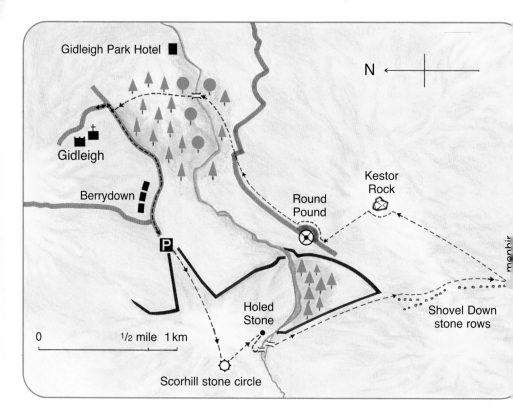

Walk 3 Scorhill, Kestor and Gidleigh

Distance: 8km Duration of walk: 2¹/₄ hours
Character: Pleasantly varied: open moorland, woodland, some
farmland, many prehistoric antiquities and a castle.

Park at 661877. A gate leads onto the moor. Head for the top of the
hill ahead of you, then follow a path down. When it forks, bear right
and in 200m you will reach Scorhill stone circle, one of the most
evocative monuments on the Moor.

Now head for the nearest corner of the conifer plantation. Cross a
stream and keep left down a path, then over some clitter (rocks). Just
opposite the point where the plantation wall meets the North Teign
(655871) is the Holed Stone, which was once thought to have curative
properties if people were passed through it. Turn right along the river
bank for 110m and two clapper bridges will take you over the stream.
Then bear left along the side of the plantation. After 1km, at the end
of the plantation, bear right uphill. Two stones standing nearly waist-
high mark the foot of the first of the Shovel Down stone rows, though
this has been heavily robbed. Proceed uphill and the row gets more

8

One of the Shovel Down stone rows, with a multi-ringed cairn circle

impressive, ending in a multi-ringed cairn circle – at which point another row starts in a different direction! Follow this row up, then carry on beyond it till you come to a gigantic menhir at 660857.

Now turn back sharply to your left and head for the rocky bulk of Kestor (665863). Circle around to the left of the tor until you see a broad path running downhill to the left. As you walk down it you will pass through the ruined field walls and huts of a village 3500 years old. Turn right along the lane. After 100 m you pass the Round Pound on your left, with a large hut circle within it. Continue along the lane, cross a cattle grid and at 669873, where the lane turns right, take the footpath on the left signed GIDLEIGH. The path is very well signpost-ed through the wooded grounds of Gidleigh Park Hotel. Cross the river, turn right and then left uphill.

Eventually you will emerge onto a lane at 672883. You could if you like cut the walk short by turning left (saving perhaps 800 m) but unless you are tired or short of time I recommend turning right, then left at a road junction, into Gidleigh with its church and miniature castle. Then retrace your steps to 672883, where you joined the lane.

Continue up the lane. Beyond Berrydown take the left turn (marked as a dead end) and it will take you back to your car.

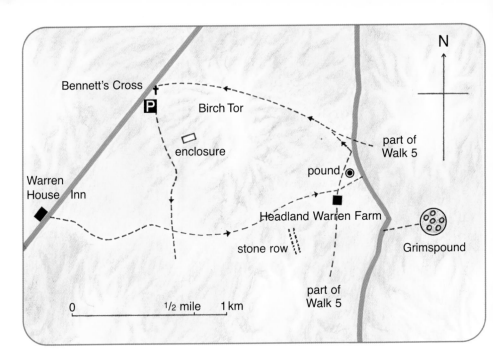

Walk 4 Vitifer Mine and Headland Warren

Distance: 4km   Duration of walk: 1¹/₄ hours.
Character: Open moorland, heavily worked by tinners.

Park at Bennett's Cross (681817). The old cross, crudely carved and very distinctive, marked a parish boundary, and perhaps also a medieval track from Chagford or Moretonhampstead to Postbridge. Start by heading almost due south from the car park (not following the most obvious track which leads south-east to Birch Tor) down towards the valley bottom. You are passing through the remains of a major mining site where in Victorian times 150 men were employed, with a mass of buildings, diggings and eight large water wheels.

The area is a Site of Special Scientific Interest because the old diggings are full of unusual lichens and many other plant species. Please keep to the track as far as possible, as the area is in danger of erosion, and be aware that these derelict mineral workings are full of hazards.

Follow the path down to the bottom of the valley and turn right. Proceed for 100m or so and you will come to the remains of substantial buildings, and on the right a very deep, narrow pit (682812) which was once home to a huge water wheel powering many of the operations on this site. Keep children and dogs under control, as you won't want to go swimming in it to rescue them! Notice the little bridge over the leat which brought the water to the wheel.

Headland Warren Farm, with the parallel 'girts' very clearly visible behind it. You will be walking between the girts towards the camera

Cross a small stream and continue to follow the path until it joins a track. After 30 m keep left at a junction of tracks. You will reach a grassy area where the track again forks. Once again take the left fork, slightly uphill towards the lowest point in the skyline on your left: you are now turning east, away from Soussons Down forestry plantation.

After 200 m you will pass an enclosure wall immediately on your right. Notice the enormous size of some of the stones. How on earth did they get them into the correct position? Continue along the path up the hill. To your right and left, parallel to the path, is a series of massive 'girts' – mining gulleys. As you reach the brow of the hill you will see Headland Warren Farm ahead and slightly to the right. When it comes into view, face 90° to the right and you should see (provided the summer vegetation is not too high) a Bronze Age double stone row climbing away from you on the hill opposite.

From around the time when the tin industry took over this area, probably c1750 but maybe earlier, the area was used as a large rabbit warren – hence the names of the farm and the Warren House Inn.

At Headland Warren Farm, start by taking the path up towards the road. Then 30 m after the signpost bear left, cross a girt and bear right up a hollow way – an ancient cart or sled track – which is the official bridleway even now. You will pass an old pound still used for collecting animals. Just before the hollow way joins the road (at 695815) it is crossed by a well-trodden path.

Turn left along it and join the Two Moors Way. As you reach the crest of Birch Tor you will see the bleakness of the high moors and ahead of you the welcome of one of England's loneliest inns – the Warren House. Your car should be visible beside the road.

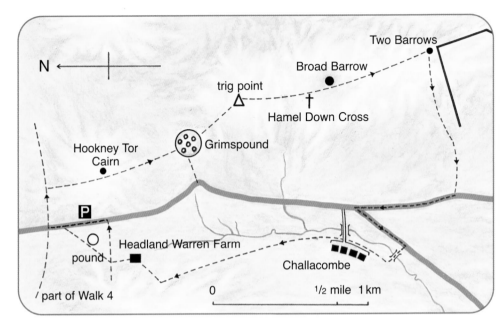

Walk 5 Grimspound and Challacombe

Distance: 7.5km   Duration of walk: 2 hours
Character: Open high moorland, then moorland valley.

Park beside the road in an old quarry at 695814. Across the valley you'll see massive scars on the hillside – the remains of tinworking in the 18th and 19th centuries – and in the valley bottom the roofs of Headland Warren Farm – once the Birch Tor Inn, serving the miners.

Walk uphill along the road for approximately 150m. Just beyond a derelict field wall, a path leads off to the right. Follow it alongside the wall. At the top of the slope you'll see a better maintained wall. Turn right here, taking the right fork towards the summit of the hill called Hookney Tor, where a substantial cairn competes for attention with granite outcrops. Below you on the slope of the next hill (Hameldown Tor) you will see Grimspound with its massive surrounding wall – a Bronze Age village. It can get busy, but as I write the whole scene is totally deserted apart from a family of ponies and a very noisy skylark.

Proceed to the village and explore the hut circles. When you have looked around to your fill, go to the uphill, south, gate of the wall and take the path up the hill, south-south-east. At the top of Hameldown Tor you'll find a cairn and a trig point from which there are amazing views, including the sea to the south-east. The track now becomes broad and well marked. Some distance further on you will see the remains of a medieval cross, perhaps 600 years old, to the right of the

The ruins of a medieval longhouse at Challacombe, probably the manor house of the medieval village

track. But the route was by then already ancient, as is suggested by the line of barrows and cairns on the highly visible skyline alongside the ancient ridgeway. Were these the graves of the lords of Grimspound in the Bronze Age, growing rich on producing tin from which the bronze was made? Broad Barrow at 706799 lives up to its name.

Continue along the level track and at 707792 you will find another barrow, with a stone sign mysteriously naming it TWO BURROWS. At this point turn right alongside a field wall, later a fence, and descend into the valley. (This field boundary is 3500 years old!) If it gets spongy underfoot, move further from the wall. You will come to a stile at the bottom of the slope from which a footpath leads on in the same direction, down to the road. Turn right along the road. The farm and neighbouring cottages are on the site of the medieval village of Challacombe. On the hillside above and north of the present settlement you can see the remains – when the light is right – of the medieval strip fields and lynchets. Turn left at the road junction. After 350 m, cross a stile on the right (at 693792) and then a bridge over the stream. Walk past the front of the farm. You will also pass the substantial remains of a medieval long house. Animals were kept in the room at the lower end and you can still see the drain through which the excrement was flushed. The family lived at the upper end.

The bridle path then proceeds through a gate and in front of the cottages. Go through another gate, then keep to the right of a ruined wall. The path is fairly clear, running parallel to the river. You'll find much evidence of tin working, dating mainly from the 19th century but the area was last worked in 1927. The bridleway passes through the farmyard; then at the junction of paths take the track to the right, up to the road. Turn left and you will soon reach your car.

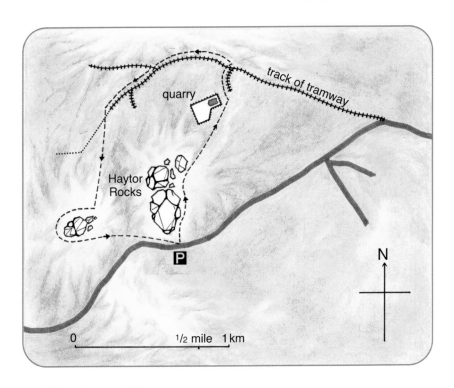

Walk 6 Around Haytor

Distance: 4.5 km   Duration of walk: 1¹/₄ hours
Character: Easy walking, industrial remains amid lovely scenery.

Park in the large car park nearest the rocks (760767). If you are coming from Bovey Tracey, it is the second car park beyond the one with a National Park Information Centre.

Cross the road and walk towards the round helmet-shaped tor. Skirt round to the right side of the rock and enjoy the view (or climb it if so inclined).

Now take the path which leads downhill to your right (045°, i.e. NE). After approximately 200 m you will see to your left a wire fence which conceals the first signs that this delightful moorland was once the scene of major industrial activity. This is the Haytor Quarry which supplied granite for many of London's buildings, including the 1832 London Bridge. It is a sheltered spot with a pool which attracts school parties for pond dipping, etc.

Follow the fence round and you will find a gate which allows you to explore the quarry if you wish. Otherwise, proceed straight on to the lower end of the man-made gulley along which stone was removed from the quarry.

A small abandoned quarry near Haytor

At the end of the gulley turn left along a very distinctive track with granite kerbs to either side. This was part of the Haytor granite tramway built in 1820. Follow it as it curves round to the right and across a causeway until you come to a junction of two tracks with a set of points also constructed from granite. A hole in the granite was the hinge for the moving part of the points. Turn sharp left here, taking you back on the new line. (Haytor will now be to your left.)

Follow the gentle uphill gradient as the track climbs towards other quarries. Three sets of points take branches to the right: ignore them. Then take the first branch to the left. The granite track is hardly recognisable at this stage, but a footpath leads you through the gorse. Take a line between Haytor itself on the left and the outcrop of rocks on your right. Once you are more or less level with the small tor on your right, follow the path which leads upwards to its left-hand side; 40 m short of the small tor, take a lesser track to its right into several disused quarries which are worth exploring.

Now circle anti-clockwise around to the southern edge of the small tor and you should again be able to see Haytor, with a broad track leading towards it, initially downhill. At a fork in the track you can decide either to climb the tor itself or keep right towards the road and the car park which you should see clearly ahead of you.

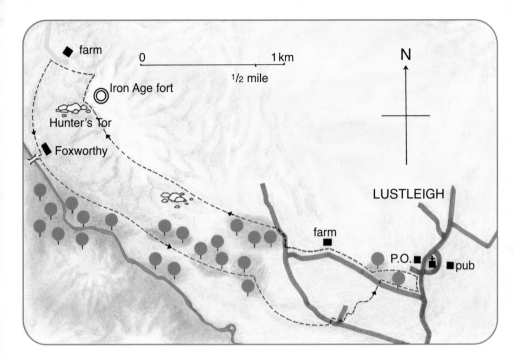

Walk 7 Lustleigh Cleave

Distance: 8.35 km   Duration of walk: nearly 3 hours
Character: The longest and most demanding walk in this book, with
strenuous gradients. Woodland valley with rocky outcrops.

Park in the centre of Lustleigh. Start by the post office (785813) and walk down a short road past the village hall to Lustleigh Town Orchard. Go through the orchard across a stream and up a hill. At a junction of paths, take the middle one which climbs at the steepest gradient. This soon brings you to a little-used lane. Turn right along it, up a steep hill and through an attractive cluster of farm buildings. At a T-junction of lanes, turn right. After 180 m take a footpath on the left (between houses called 'Logan Stones' and 'Grove'). Pass through a gate and take the bridleway straight ahead, signposted 'HUNTER'S TOR'.

This is a long climb through woodland and between massive granite boulders in places, and is best not attempted after a heavy lunch! When you finally reach the top of the hill, the woodland opens out and there are ferns as well as trees, and you realise you are walking along a ridge above a steep-sided valley – the Cleave. You will reach an impressive tor overhanging the cliff edge: this is called Harton Chest.

The path continues to wind gently uphill until by 300 m altitude there are very few trees, even short scrubby ones. Just before you reach

16

*Harton
Chest,
overlooking
Lustleigh
Cleave*

a wall across the path, leading to a tor overhanging the valley, you will be passing on your right Hunter's Tor, an Iron Age fort – but don't be surprised if you can't even find it.

Go through the gate (761825), turn right and follow the footpath downhill. When it reaches a track, turn left. Go through one gate, turn right through another, and down the side of the field, keeping the farm on your right; then through another gate and follow the concrete farm track. Where it bears round to the right, turn left through a gate signposted 'FOXWORTHY BRIDGE'.

The path goes through a gate and becomes a delightful old Devon lane. Celia Fiennes in the 17th century grumbled that Devon's main roads were like this – she was describing what is now the A38. Further gates bring you to the hamlet of Foxworthy. Stay this side of the river and turn left on the bridlepath signposted 'HAMMERSLAKE'.

At a junction of paths, keep left, signposted 'HAMMERSLAKE FOR LUSTLEIGH'. The path climbs gently but persistently up the slope of the cleave until it forks: take the right fork along the level contour. At a T-junction of paths, turn right, signed 'MANATON VIA WATER'. Follow this downhill until another junction where you carry straight on, signed 'LUSTLEIGH VIA PETHY BRIDGE'. Follow the main path, generally straight on, and follow the next sign for Lustleigh, then keep left uphill.

Once through a gate, the path becomes a track which emerges on to a lane. Turn right along this and in 50 m left, along another lane ('Pethybridge'), passing a magnificent thatched long-house. Then turn right immediately beside it (noticing the thatch extending to within a metre of the ground on the lean-to at the rear of the house) between several other thatched buildings and follow the lane down; turn left at a chapel, back into the centre of the village.

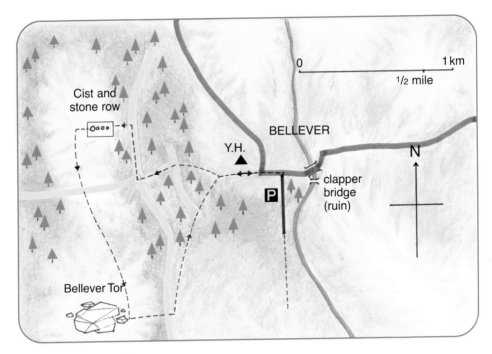

Cist and stone row

BELLEVER

Y.H.

clapper bridge (ruin)

N

0   1 km

1/2 mile

Bellever Tor

Walk 8 Bellever

Distance: 5 km   Duration of walk: 1¹/2 hours
Character: Conifer plantations and fairly open moorland.

Park at 656772. Leave the car park by the track back to the road and turn left along it. At the junction, walk straight ahead past the Youth Hostel along the Lichway path – initially a tarmac lane, then a track heading sharply uphill through a gate and becoming a stony path.

Go through a second field gate and turn right along the edge of the woodland. Cross a forest track at 650774. At the next junction, where five tracks meet, turn right. After 300 m along this track, where it dips slightly, there is a path to the left: this brings you after 120 m to a particularly beautiful short stone row and well preserved cist at 645776. In 2002 this area had been recently felled. The stone row itself stands in a wire enclosure. Go through this and out the other side.

Once in the grassland area, turn left and head south for Bellever Tor. A well walked path heads to the left of the tor near a walled wood, and then bears back towards the summit. (The settlement and field system shown on the OS map are not among Dartmoor's more spectacular and you may not think them worth a detour.)

Descend from the summit of the tor by a path which runs approximately east and descends to a gap in a wall at 647765. There is a

A short stone row and cist, surrounded by forestry. The nearby trees had recently been felled when this photograph was taken

The view northwards from Bellever Tor

bench here which will serve as a landmark or a resting place as you wish!

Continue down a rocky path for 50 m until you meet a forest track. Turn left then immediately bear right along a broad and easy forestry path. Unlike some routes through conifer plantations, this is not especially gloomy!

At 651771 you will find a turning circle for forestry lorries, with the main forestry track bearing off to the left. You go straight on down a path which after 150 m comes to a gate. Here you rejoin the outward track and make your way back to the car park – with perhaps a brief detour down to the clapper bridge.

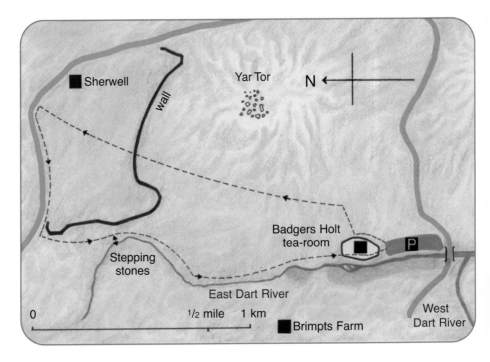

Walk 9 From Dartmeet

Distance: 4.8 km   Duration of walk: 1 1/2 hours
Character: Hillside with pleasant views, then idyllic river valley. This is
a walk which varies in character according to the conditions underfoot.
It's an easy stroll after dry weather but a wet spell can make it quite
hard going in places, with waterproof footwear and a degree of agility
required.

Park in the large car park at 673733. Walk through the car park towards
the Badgers Holt tea-room. Just before the restaurant signs, bear right
through a gate along a footpath. This passes around the tea-room
complex, leading to some superb picnic sites alongside the West Dart
river. However, your path leads off to the right, about half way around
the complex, up quite a steep slope.

After climbing for approximately 120 m, a narrow path to your left
leads almost along the contour, but climbs gradually. This can be
obscured by bracken and prickly gorse in summer, but if you follow
the contour until you are opposite Brimpts Farm across the valley, you
will then see several thorn trees ahead of you. Make for a point just
uphill from these and you will find that several sheeptracks join to
form more of a main path, which then starts to climb a little more
steeply up the hill.

The East Dart River, just north of Badgers Holt

For the whole of this stretch the OS map shows a path which I have yet to find on the ground! However, if you follow its general trend, and when in doubt go uphill rather than down, you should come to an enclosure wall, with a gate and stile at 677745.

Cross the stile and go down the edge of the field, noting the old settlement of Sherwell ahead of you. Carry on down to a foot bridge across a stream, through two fields, and finally out through a stile on to a tarmac lane: turn left along it.

When the hill flattens out, just before a passing bay, turn left along a footpath. This leads down into the valley of the East Dart, with a tributary running alongside the path. You will reach a clapper bridge at 672749. As a diversion, you can cross the clapper and turn left, down to the main river where there is a ford with tall stepping stones beside it and a bridleway leading up to Brimpts. For this walk, though, we return to the clapper and make our way along the left bank of the stream and then of the East Dart, returning to Badgers Holt beside the river. A fair amount of scrambling across boulders and through marshy brooks is required on this route after wet weather. But the tearoom awaits you!

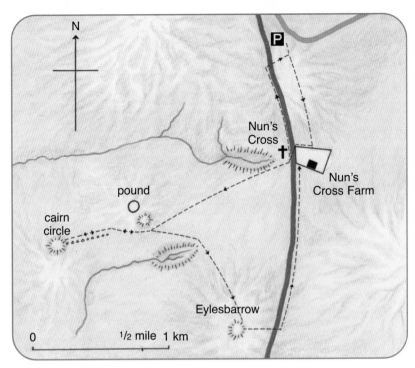

Walk 10 Nun's Cross and Hingston Hill stone row

Distance: 6.5 km   Duration of walk: 1³/4 hours
Character: Open moorland. Compass and map vital.

Park at 604708 and take the track which bears right from the road and runs almost due south, keeping the contour while the road descends to the left. The low ground to your left is Fox Tor Mire, famous as the setting for the conclusion of *Hound of the Baskervilles*. The metalled track brings you to a field wall, the edge of abandoned Nun's Cross Farm, a 'newtake' of the 1860s. Turn right alongside a newtake wall, noticing how the land just inside has been worked, presumably for tin, leaving great scars on the otherwise smooth surface of the moor.

When the field wall ends, turn left along the major walking track and you will soon come to Nun's Cross, also known as Siward's Cross (604699). From this point, take a compass bearing of 250° and keep walking for 200 m. When you come to a tin-streaming valley, head up above it on the left-hand side and you may well find signs of tracks in the grass leading towards a very prominent crag and hill in the distance – Sheepstor. You can now aim for Sheepstor.

The path gradually becomes more distinct until you reach a Bronze Age cairn at 592695. Some stone has been carted away but you can still see it was a real building, by no means just a heap of stones.

Towards Sheepstor you can see the Hingston Hill stone row. Walk along the row to the stone circle at the far end: actually it is probably the remains of another huge cairn, robbed of all its smaller stones and so leaving the outer ring looking like a stone circle (587693).

Return along the stone row to the cairn at the eastern end. As you near the cairn, you will notice on your left a pound – a stone-walled enclosure of unknown age. From the cairn take a compass bearing of 140° and you will see a rounded hill. Head for the top of this hill, probably skirting the tinner's girt which is in your direct path. This is quite a long climb with glorious views across open moorland – tussocky grass and heather in places, so not easy going. As you near the top of the hill, you may come across assay pits – test pits which the miners dug in their search for the ore-bearing lodes.

On the summit of the hill are two Bronze Age cairns, a boundary marker for the Burrator reservoir catchment area ('PCWW 1917'), and a much older boundary stone. The larger cairn is Eylesbarrow, and it was a boundary of the 'Forest' of Dartmoor.

Now head down in an approximately easterly direction and you will meet a well-maintained long distance walkers' path. Turn left along this and it will take you back to Nun's Cross: carry on along the path for a further 550 m. You will come to a kink in the path by a large rock, with another path crossing it. Turn right here. When you reach a T-junction, turn left along the track and you will arrive back at your car.

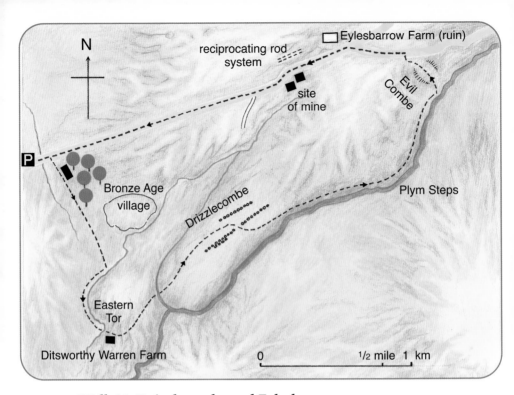

Walk 11 Drizzlecombe and Eylesbarrow

Distance: 7.5 km   Duration of walk: 2 hours
Character: Open moor, very lonely in places. Compass and map vital.

Park at Nattor (578673). Walk down to the bridge and cross towards
the conifers up a stony track. Bear right through a gate ('PUBLIC BRIDLE-
PATH'), passing the front of a building, then through another gate on
to the open moor. A reasonably well defined track leads towards a tor
just below the horizon (heading 150°). To your right are characteristic
signs of tin streaming. As these end, the path forks. Take the left fork
towards the top of the hill, until you reach a leat. Follow this round to
the right till you reach Ditsworthy Warren Farm. Follow the cart track
which runs from the back of the abandoned farm, behind Eastern Tor.

Ahead of you, you should see the Drizzlecombe stone rows. Carry
on until the track crosses a stream, then head for the nearest menhir.

The Drizzlecombe ceremonial complex consists of three long stone
rows, each with a huge menhir (the tallest being 4.2 m high), 22 asso-
ciated cairns and other stone settings. It was probably constructed
3500-4000 years ago. Several other ceremonial complexes lie within
an hour or two's walk, so this was hardly the equivalent of a medieval
cathedral, more like the parish church of a prosperous village.

The lonely upper reaches of the River Plym. In this part of the walk I have never yet met another walker...

Bear right from the tallest menhir, up the Plym valley. (You may wish to explore the cairns at the top of the row before joining this path.) Follow the path parallel to the stream – the upper reaches of the River Plym, which at this point is very attractive but little walked.

Shortly after Langcombe Brook joins the Plym from the opposite side of the stream, you reach Plym Steps (603672) – an old fording point – where you stay on the left side of the stream and follow the bend round to the left. After 500 m you will reach a point where the valley bottom broadens. Follow a line between the boggy ground on your right and the clitter (granite boulders) on your left till you reach a point where a dry valley heads to your left. Follow the left slope of this valley, called Evil Combe, with clear signs of old spoil heaps and, at the top of the valley, girts (gullies where a tin lode has been worked).

At the top of the girt you will find a track. At this point you should head north west. Almost immediately you'll see some ruins and a little knoll on the hillside ahead of you. Head for that and you will find a broad track along which you turn left. This is your route all the way back (unless you decide to explore the Bronze Age village).

The ruins you pass through are those of an early 19th century farm with outbuildings and field enclosures. Downhill from the farm you pass through the remains of a substantial tin mine known as Eylesbarrow, which closed in 1852 and which you may wish to explore. Parallel to the track and to the right of it is what looks at first like a stone row but is actually the base of a reciprocating rod system, which transferred power from a water-wheel to pumps and machinery.

At the fork in the tracks, take the main track to the right which will bring you back to your car.

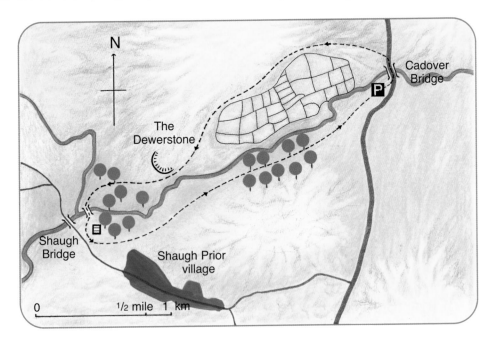

Walk 12 The Dewerstone

Distance: 6.5 km   Duration of walk: 1 3/4 hours
Character: Initially on grazing land, then woodland.

Park in the large car park at Cadover Bridge (555645). Cross to the north side of the bridge and immediately turn left on to a farm track. Within 15 m bear right up the hill towards an old cross, about 300 m away. Continue uphill, keeping the field boundary on your left.

The path you want skirts the enclosures on your left, never far from the field boundary. You will pass a huge chunk of granite split in two. This was done deliberately and you can see the marks of the 'feather and tare' wedges in the top edge.

When, after 1 km, the wall starts to veer away to your left, carry on more or less in a straight line (south-west): in good visibility you'll see Plymouth Sound directly ahead. You should come to a small tor. Ahead of you is the Dewerstone (Dewer is dialect for Devil) – a distinctive rounded hill with rocky outcrops on its left side. The path to it is generally well walked and easy to follow.

The hill was fortified during the centuries immediately before the arrival of the Romans and a few signs of these fortifications remain. The main path runs to the left of the tor, then begins to descend to the great granite outcrops which overhang the valley, surrounded by stunted and lichen-covered oak trees. A well-worn path descends through the wood: it is quite steep and can be a scramble in places.

Less than half way down to the river, turn right along a stony path which will lead you gently downwards. When you reach a junction, turn sharp left downhill on a granite-paved path which soon turns back to the right. A notice board on the left indicates a path to the foot of the Dewerstone crags, much favoured by rock climbers. Go straight on here. Further downhill, a wooden footbridge crosses the Plym at the point where it meets the Meavy. On the other side of the bridge, beside a massive industrial building in ruins, there is a car park.

At the right-hand side of the ruins, which were once a china clay 'dry', a flight of steps leads upwards past another range of buildings and back to the road – but a footpath leads off to the left at this point, up through a bluebell wood. Cross a stile and continue uphill, bearing right after 20 m. When you have climbed through the wood and reached a field (bracken-covered in summer), proceed up its left side towards a house ahead of you, on the outskirts of Shaugh Prior.

The path bears off to the left along the top edge of the valley, with views of the Dewerstone on the opposite side. This path is known as the Pipe Walk and you will soon see why. Straight on at the junction of paths. A large structure to the left was once a water storage tank.

All the while, to your left and below you, you will see and hear the rushing stream of the River Plym as it descends across rapids. Pass through North Wood (NT), then traverse a little obstacle course, including a wooden ladder (only four steps!). Continue following the Pipe Walk which runs more or less at a level, coming ever closer to the stream until you reach the car park at Cadover Bridge.

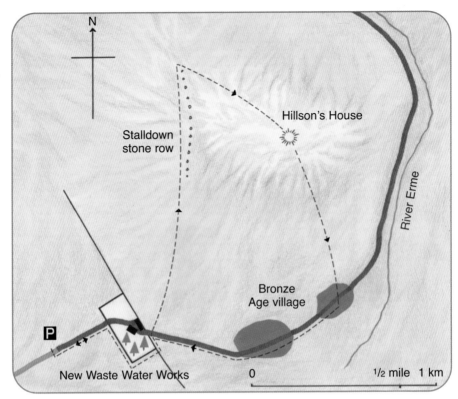

Walk 13 Stalldown Stone Row

Distance: 5.5 km   Duration of walk: 1¹/₂ hours
Character: A relatively short walk for a taste of open moorland and
some interesting antiquities. Compass and map needed.

Park at the entrance to New Waste Water Works (626612). Walk up
the concrete track and round to the right of the water works ('PUBLIC
ACCESS TO ERME VALLEY'). At the end of the fenced enclosure turn left
and enter the moor by a stile. Turn left along the wall till you come to
a track. Take a compass bearing of 015° – it's approximately 80° to the
left of the line of the track – and head uphill crossing a dry leat. It is a
short but strenuous climb and should bring you to a point due south
of the Stalldown stone row, which climbs up to the horizon. The
stones near the summit are tall enough to stand out in silhouette even
at some distance – no doubt intentionally.

Look out to your right from these tall stones and you will see the
valley of the Erme, which was once full of Bronze Age settlements: in
those days the weather was several degrees warmer and the moor
more hospitable. Then look a little further to the right and on the near
skyline you will see a cairn, with a path leading to it.

28

The Stalldown stone row

This is 'Hillson's House'. It is said that Hillson was an 18th century clock maker who built himself a hut in the ruins of the ancient cairn. Apparently clock-making was once a rural winter occupation, and it was not unusual for Dartmoor people to build their own dwellings, so perhaps the story is true! Notice how spongy the ground is as you walk towards the cairn. The upper parts of Dartmoor absorb the winter rains and gradually release them through the summer, ensuring that the rivers always run plentifully.

At Hillson's House bear slightly to the right and continue down towards the valley. If you have a compass, a bearing of 160° will take you down the hillside until you reach a track which runs parallel to the stream some 140 m lower in altitude than Hillson's House. As you descend the slope you will notice that the river Erme runs into a wooded area in the distance. Head for the point where you see it disappearing into the woodland. This line will take you into the ruins of a Bronze Age village. You should be able to spot round houses and numerous enclosures. Like most such sites, it is at its best in winter and spring, before the bracken grows up and obscures it.

Descend though the village to the track and turn right along it. It will bring you back to the five-barred gate and the stile at the water works – named, incidentally, from the New Waste, not waste-water!

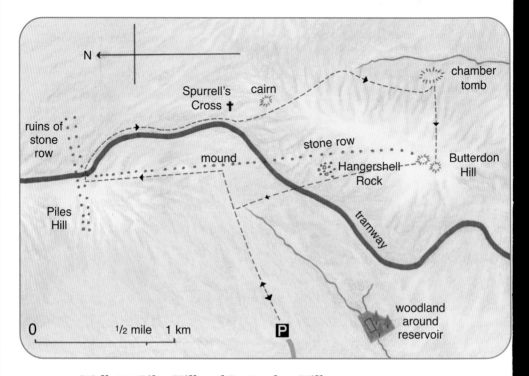

Walk 14 Piles Hill and Butterdon Hill

Distance: 8.5 km   Duration of walk: 2¹/₄ hours
Character: Open moorland. Compass and map essential.

Park at Harford Moor Gate (643596). With your back to the gate, head straight on in the direction of the road (bearing 070°). Once you have crossed the brow of the hill, you will see on the skyline ahead of you a small tor to the right and a long low mound to the left.

Cross the stream where you can – after heavy rain keep to the left of the direct line – and continue up to the mound. Twenty metres short of it (at 656596) you will cross a path which runs alongside the Butterdon Hill stone row – not immediately impressive because the stones are small, but it extends for 2 km, the second longest on Dartmoor.

Turn left at the stone row and walk north along it. In this area there are numerous cairns and indeed small stone rows. Continue straight on up the hill and at the top you will find a menhir next to a much later boundary stone, creating a curious parent and child effect.

At the next boundary stone you join up with the line of the Red Lake tramway. Running east-west at this point (654611), but initially almost invisible, is the Piles Hill stone row. If this were intact it would apparently have been the most impressive and perhaps the oldest on